TONI MORRISON

POWER OF THE PEN

BLACK WOMEN WRITERS

by Joyce Markovics

NORWOOD HOUSE PRESS

NORWOOD HOUSE PRESS

For more information about Norwood House Press, please visit our website at: www.norwoodhousepress.com or call 866-565-2900.

Book Designer: Ed Morgan
Editorial and Production: Bowerbird Books

Photo Credits: Wikimedia Commons, cover and title page; © Dennis Van Tine/LFI/Photoshot/Newscom, 5; Wikimedia Commons, 6; Courtesy of the Lorain Public Library System, 7, 8, 9, 10; Wikimedia Commons/Derek E. Morton, 11; Wikimedia Commons, 12; Library of Congress/Bernard Gotfryd collection, 13; Library of Congress/Bernard Gotfryd collection, 14; Wikimedia Commons/Zarateman, 15; © Dimitris Legakiss/Splash News/Newscom, 16; © spatuletail/Shutterstock, 17; © On The Run Photo/Shutterstock, 18; © KEN REGAN/KRT/Newscom, 19; © KEIVN DIETSCH/UPI/Newscom, 21.

Copyright © 2024 Norwood House Press

Hardcover ISBN: 978-1-68450-671-2
Paperback ISBN: 978-1-68404-974-5

All rights reserved. No part of this book may be reproduced or utilized in any form or by any means without written permission from the publisher.

Library of Congress Cataloging-in-Publication Data

Names: Markovics, Joyce L., author.
Title: Toni Morrison / by Joyce Markovics.
Description: Buffalo : Norwood House Press, 2024. | Series: Power of the pen: Black women writers | Includes bibliographical references and index. | Audience: Grades 4-6
Identifiers: LCCN 2023045985 (print) | LCCN 2023045986 (ebook) | ISBN 9781684506712 (hardcover) | ISBN 9781684049745 (paperback) | ISBN 9781684049806 (ebook)
Subjects: LCSH: Morrison, Toni--Juvenile literature. | Novelists, American--20th century--Biography--Juvenile literature. | African American women novelists--20th century--Biography--Juvenile literature. | LCGFT: Biographies. | Picture books.
Classification: LCC PS3563.O8749 Z758 2024 (print) | LCC PS3563.O8749 (ebook) | DDC 813/.54 [B]--dc23/eng/20231002
LC record available at https://lccn.loc.gov/2023045985
LC ebook record available at https://lccn.loc.gov/2023045986

372N--012024

Manufactured in the United States of America in North Mankato, Minnesota.

CONTENTS

Introducing Toni 4
Early Years 6
Her Work 12
Toni's Power 20

Timeline and Activity 22
Glossary 23
For More Information 24
Index 24
About the Author 24

INTRODUCING TONI

> *My world did not shrink because I was a Black female writer. It just got bigger.*

Toni Morrison moved people with her words. She was an **editor**, a writer, and a teacher who loved language. And Toni used it in powerful ways. She wrote about the experiences of Black people, especially women. She saw her novels as tools for remembering the past. "For me the history of the place of Black people in this country is so varied, complex and beautiful. And impactful," Toni said. Until she died, Toni challenged herself to be better—and to make the world better.

ASK YOURSELF
WHY IS THE PAST IMPORTANT? HOW IS IT PART OF THE PRESENT?

Toni Morrison was an influential American writer.

TONI RECEIVED THE NOBEL PRIZE IN 1993. THIS PRIZE HONORS PEOPLE WHO HAVE DONE GREAT WORK. IT'S ONE OF THE MOST IMPORTANT AWARDS THAT ANYBODY CAN RECEIVE.

EARLY YEARS

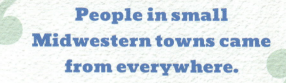

"People in small Midwestern towns came from everywhere."

On February 18, 1931, Toni Morrison was born in Lorain, Ohio. Her birth name was Chloe Ardelia Wofford. She was the second of four children. Her parents were George and Ella. Both came from the South. They moved north to escape **racism** and to build a better life. There were Black, brown, and white people in Lorain. "We all played together," said Toni. And everybody was poor. As a child, Toni thought "the whole world was like Lorain."

This ship was built in Lorain, Ohio, which is located near Lake Erie.

Toni's father George worked many jobs. One was as a welder in a shipyard. He was proud of his work. George would sometimes sign the ships he helped build. Still, he struggled to support his family. Once, when George couldn't pay rent, the landlord set the Wofford's house on fire. Toni remembers that day. It was a "bizarre form of evil," she said.

This is Toni as a small child. She changed her name from Chloe to Toni in college.

BECAUSE OF LAWS IN THE SOUTH, BLACK PEOPLE WERE FORCED TO LIVE APART FROM WHITES. THESE RACIST LAWS LASTED UNTIL 1965. RACIST LAWS ALSO EXISTED IN THE NORTH BUT WERE LESS HARSH.

> **Being able to laugh got me through.**

Toni's mother Ella sang in the church choir. She was kind but fierce. When Black people weren't allowed to sit in parts of the movie theater, Ella marched in and sat down. She often wrote letters—even to the president—in support of what was right. "My mother believed something should be done about **inhuman** situations," said Toni.

ASK YOURSELF
HOW DO JOY AND LAUGHTER HELP YOU DEAL WITH HARD TIMES?

Mother and daughter, Ella and Toni

Despite many hardships, the Wofford house was happy. It overflowed with laughter, music, and stories. As a child, Toni's family shared **folklore**, including ghost stories. "My father's were the best . . . the scariest," she said. Toni's family also treasured books. Toni learned to read at an early age. In first grade, Toni was the only kid in her class who could read.

This is Toni's first home in Lorain.

> **"What's the world for you if you can't make it up the way you want it?"**

Reading helped Toni in school. She was always at the top of her class. She grew to love the writers Jane Austen and Leo Tolstoy. In high school, Toni was on the **debate** team and in the drama club. Also, she worked on her high school yearbook and newspaper. Still, Toni dreamed of a place with more Black people like her.

Toni (front center) works on her high school's newspaper.

AFTER SCHOOL, TONI WORKED TO HELP OUT HER FAMILY. AT ONE JOB, SHE CLEANED A WHITE FAMILY'S HOUSE. TONI HATED THE WORK. HER FATHER TOLD HER, "YOU DON'T LIVE THERE. YOU LIVE *HERE*." TONI LEARNED SHE WAS NOT DEFINED BY A JOB OR BY ANYTHING ELSE.

In 1949, Toni went to Howard University, a historically Black college. "On the campus, I felt safe and welcome," said Toni. Yet she saw how people of color were judged based on their skin tone. Light-skinned people were often treated better. "It was stunning to me," she said. She studied English and drama. On stage, Toni said, "Excellence had nothing to do with color. It had only to do with talent."

Howard University is located in Washington, DC, and dates from 1867. It was at Howard where Toni officially stopped using her birth name Chloe.

HER WORK

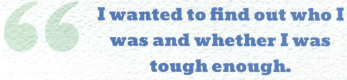

> I wanted to find out who I was and whether I was tough enough.

In 1953, Toni graduated from Howard. Then she went to Cornell University in Ithaca, New York. There, Toni earned a **master's degree**. After, she taught English at a university in Texas. "Once I got into it [teaching], I really enjoyed it," said Toni. In 1957, she returned to Howard to teach. Soon after, she met Harold Morrison, an architect. They married in 1958.

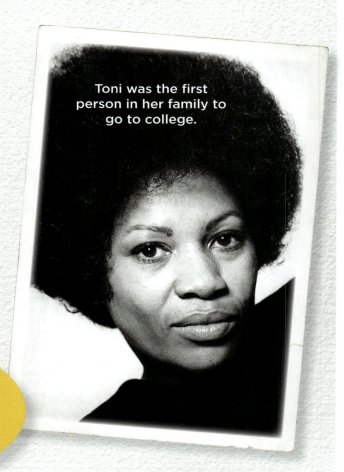

Toni was the first person in her family to go to college.

ASK YOURSELF
WHY DO YOU THINK TEACHERS ARE IMPORTANT? HAS A TEACHER EVER MADE YOU EXCITED ABOUT LEARNING?

Toni's first son, Harold Ford, was born in 1961. Toni kept teaching and joined a writers' group. Each week, members had to share a poem or story. One week, having written nothing, Toni jotted down a story. It was about a Black girl she knew from Lorain who prayed for blue eyes. In 1964, Toni had a second son, Slade. But her marriage crumbled. That same year, she got **divorced**. Toni got a job as an editor. In the evenings and mornings, she wrote while her sons slept.

It wasn't easy for Toni to raise her two sons, but she was determined to do it on her own. And she did.

> **If there's a book that you want to read, but it hasn't been written yet, then you must write it.**

Toni never forgot the story she came up with for her writers' group. She decided to turn it into a novel. She wove her own memories into the story. "I think most first novels are **autobiographical** in some way," she said. At the same time, Toni edited novels for her job. They were by important Black authors, such as Andrew Young, Gayl Jones, and Angela Davis. Toni wanted to bring Black **literature** to readers.

ASK YOURSELF
WHY DO YOU THINK A WRITER'S FIRST NOVEL TENDS TO BE MORE PERSONAL?

Angela Davis is a professor and author. She fights for the rights of Black people.

In 1970, Toni **published** her book. She called it *The Bluest Eye*. The book is about three Black girls. It takes place in Toni's hometown of Lorain. To escape abuse, one of the characters dreams of having blue eyes. Over time, her **obsession** leads to madness. Overall, **critics** liked the book. One said that Toni's writing could "reveal the beauty and hope below the surface."

This is a mural of Toni Morrison in Spain.

WRITING ALMOST NEVER CAME EASILY TO TONI. "YOU JUST HAVE TO LET IT GO, WAIT FOR IT TO BE THERE," SHE SAID. FOR TONI, EDITING WAS JUST AS IMPORTANT AS WRITING. "THE REVISION FOR ME IS THE EXCITING PART."

> **Freeing yourself was one thing; claiming ownership of that freed self was another.**

Toni wanted to keep telling stories about Black people's lives. She took another job teaching. And she kept writing and editing. Toni started work on her second novel, *Sula*. Because she was a busy parent, Toni mostly wrote the book in her head. "It was very difficult writing and **rearing** children," said Toni. But she figured out how to do both. In 1973, she published *Sula*. The book follows the story of two very different female friends.

Here is Toni being interviewed about her books. She felt stories should be lingered over and not "gobbled up like fast food."

ASK YOURSELF
JUGGLING MANY RESPONSIBILITIES CAN BE HARD. WHY IS TIME MANAGEMENT IMPORTANT?

After *Sula*, Toni took a break from writing. In 1974, she created *The Black Book*. Using **collage**, it explores the full history of Black Americans. She said, "It was like growing up Black one more time." Toni wanted to tell "the history of African Americans from the point of view of everyday people." She then wrote *Song of Solomon*. It came out in 1977. It was followed by *Tar Baby* in 1981. By then, Toni had become a famous writer.

In 2023, Toni was honored with a postage stamp. It was created to remind people of the power of her words and ideas.

TONI'S BOOK *TAR BABY* IS ABOUT TWO PEOPLE FROM OPPOSITE BACKGROUNDS WHO FALL IN LOVE.

> **We die. That may be the meaning of life. But we do language. That may be the measure of our lives.**

The success of her latest books allowed Toni to write full-time. She wrote essays, plays, and more novels. In 1987, she released *Beloved*. The idea for the book came from the true story of a woman who had been enslaved. Toni wanted to share the terrible truths of slavery. "I had to feel what it might feel like for my own children to be enslaved," she said. *Beloved* became a bestseller. It was praised as a masterpiece.

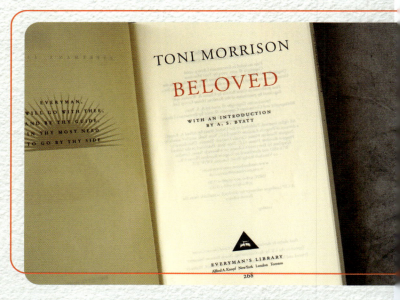

Beloved tells the story of Sethe, whose memories of being enslaved haunt her.

Toni went on to teach, speak, and write. She taught writing at Princeton University. She received hundreds of requests a year as a speaker. And Toni wrote more novels and many other works. These included children's books and even an opera! "There's a difference between writing for a living and writing for life," she said. Toni wrote for life.

Beloved was made into a movie starring Oprah Winfrey. Oprah was a big supporter of Toni's.

BELOVED WON AN IMPORTANT AWARD, THE PULITZER PRIZE FOR FICTION. NOT LONG AFTER, TONI WON THE NOBEL PRIZE IN LITERATURE. THIS WAS A FIRST FOR A BLACK WOMAN.

TONI'S POWER

> "Make a difference about something other than yourselves."

In 2010, Toni's son, Slade, died from cancer. The shock caused Toni to stop writing. Then she thought Slade would be upset if he knew his mom stopped writing. So Toni picked up her pen. Later in life, Toni dealt with health issues. A bad back made walking difficult. However, when she wrote, she was pain-free. Writing is "the place where I live," said Toni.

On August 5, 2019, Toni died in New York City. She was 88 years old. In all, Toni published 11 novels. Each one shined a light on the experiences of Black Americans. Each drew readers into Toni's rich, heartfelt stories and challenged them to "make a difference."

IN 2012, PRESIDENT BARACK OBAMA HONORED TONI WITH THE PRESIDENTIAL MEDAL OF FREEDOM.

ASK YOURSELF WHY IS IT IMPORTANT TO ALWAYS BE TRUE TO YOURSELF?

Toni receives the Presidential Medal of Freedom from President Obama.

TIMELINE AND ACTIVITY

February 18, 1931
Toni Morrison is born Chloe Ardelia Wofford in Lorain, Ohio

1953
Toni graduates from Howard University

1970
Toni publishes *The Bluest Eye*

1974
The Black Book is published

1987
Toni publishes *Beloved*

1988
She receives the Pulitzer Prize for fiction

1993
Toni wins the Nobel Prize for literature

August 5, 2019
Toni dies at age 88

GET WRITING!

Toni Morrison often based her stories on real people or events. Think of an actual person or event that moved you. How did it make you feel and why? Then write a short story about it. Share your work with an adult or friend!

GLOSSARY

autobiographical (aw-toh-bye-uh-GRAF-ih-kuhl): dealing with a person's life.

collage (kuh-LAHZH): a type of art that involves sticking various materials such as photos and newspaper clippings to a backing board.

critics (KRIT-iks): people who judge or criticize something.

debate (di-BATE): a discussion of a problem or issue.

divorced (dih-VAWRSD): no longer married.

editor (ED-ih-ter): a person in charge of the final content of a book or text.

folklore (FOHK-lor): the stories and beliefs of a group of people.

inhuman (in-HYOO-muhn): cruel and barbaric.

literature (LIT-er-uh-cher): written works.

master's degree (MAS-terz duh-GREE): a degree that's given after at least one year of graduate study.

obsession (uhb-SESH-uhn): the state of being unable to think about anything else.

published (PUHB-lishd): printed or made available for people to read.

racism (REY-siz-uhm): a system of beliefs and policies based on the idea that one race is better than another.

rearing (REER-ing): raising.

revision (rih-VIZH-uh): the act of reworking something, especially text.

FOR MORE INFORMATION

Books

Morrison, Toni and Slade. *A Toni Morrison Treasury*. New York, NY: Simon & Schuster, 2023. Read stories by Toni and her son, Slade.

O'Neill, Bill. *The Great Book of Black Heroes*. Sheridan, WY: LAK Publishing, 2021. Explore the lives of 30 incredible Black people.

Websites

Britannica Kids: Toni Morrison
(https://kids.britannica.com/students/article/Toni-Morrison/312581)
Learn about Toni Morrison's life.

The Nobel Prize: Toni Morrison
(https://www.nobelprize.org/prizes/literature/1993/morrison/biographical/)
Discover more about Toni Morrison's Nobel Prize.

INDEX

awards, 5, 19, 20
Beloved, 18, 19
The Black Book, 17
The Bluest Eye, 15
childhood, 6, 7, 8, 9, 10
college, 11
critics, 15
editor, 4, 13
father, 6, 7, 9, 10
folklore, 9
jobs, Toni's, 10, 13, 14, 16
legacy, 20
Lorain, Ohio, 6, 13, 15
mother, 6, 8
novels, 4, 14, 16, 18, 19, 20
racism, 6, 7
Song of Solomon, 17
Sula, 16, 17
Tar Baby, 17

ABOUT THE AUTHOR

Joyce Markovics has written hundreds of children's books. She's passionate about celebrating the lives and accomplishments of women. Joyce thanks Cheri Campbell and the Lorain Public Library System for generously contributing to this book.